amy tangerine

MAKing Memories

This book is about to show you
how to collect your words, thoughts,
and reflections.

Get ready to treasure your triumphs,
reflect upon the lessons you learn, and
appreciate the little things in life.

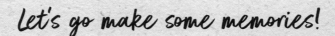

Let's go make some memories!

DK Penguin Random House

Author Amy Tangerine
Illustrator Tracey English
US Senior Editor Shannon Beatty
Editor Sophie Parkes
Senior Art Editor Rachael Parfitt Hunt
Design Assistant Sif Nørskov
Photographer Lol Johnson
Managing Editor Penny Smith
Jacket Designer Rachael Parfitt Hunt
Jacket Coordinator Issy Walsh
Production Editors Dragana Puvacic, Rob Dunn
Production Controller Magda Bojko
Publishing Director Sarah Larter
Deputy Art Director Mabel Chan

First American Edition, 2022
Published in the United States by DK Publishing
1450 Broadway, Suite 801, New York, NY 10018

Text copyright © Amy Tan 2022
Copyright © 2022 Dorling Kindersley Limited
DK, a Division of Penguin Random House LLC
22 23 24 25 26 10 9 8 7 6 5 4 3 2 1
001–321628–Jan/2022

A catalog record for this book
is available from the Library of Congress.
ISBN 978-0-7440-2655-9

DK books are available at special discounts when purchased in bulk for
sales promotions, premiums, fund-raising, or educational use. For
details, contact: DK Publishing Special Markets,
1450 Broadway, Suite 801, New York, NY 10018
SpecialSales@dk.com

Printed and bound in China

For the curious
www.dk.com

MIX
Paper from
responsible sources
FSC™ C018179

This book was made with Forest
Stewardship Council™ certified paper –
one small step in DK's commitment to
a sustainable future. For more information
go to www.dk.com/our-green-pledge

Contents

Hello friend!

Welcome to your making memories journey! I believe that everyone is creative and has a story to tell. I hope that this book can help you tell it.

Through the process of recording my life on paper, whether through scrapbooking or journaling, since I was 10 years old, I have learned a lot about life and most importantly, myself. Now, as a person who designs and plays with art supplies for my job, I love sharing my passion for making memories, achieving your goals, and having fun along the way.

This book will show you how to scrapbook, journal, and craft in order to record your memories and remind you of the good things in your life. It will guide you through activities to make you feel calm and chill, to help you connect with your feelings and the world around you, and to appreciate the little things in life.

My hope for this book is that it inspires you to live joyfully and fully in the moment. Cherish the things that matter. And remember, the only rule is to be open-minded and have fun!

amy tangerine

Mindfulness and making memories

It can be easy to rush through life without noticing the beautiful little things. This book will show you how to be present in the moment, experience life fully, and make memories of the things you do.

This is called mindfulness. It involves paying attention to your thoughts and feelings and the world around you. You can be mindful at any time, no matter who you are, where you are, or what you are doing.

Throughout this book, you will find ideas, activities, and tips that will help you do this.

You should find being mindful helps you to understand yourself better and to cherish elements of the world around you that you hadn't appreciated before. It might help you to see yourself and your life in a happy way, and means you'll be more likely to remember the good things that happen because you are fully living in the moment when they do.

Mindfulness is great for your mental health. It helps reduce stress and anxiety, makes you feel calm, and can help you understand the thoughts and emotions that influence your behavior, too.

An elephant never forgets!

Throughout this book you will find a little elephant. Elephants are strong, patient animals with a talent for remembering. You may have heard the saying "an elephant never forgets." While this is a slight exaggeration, it has been shown that certain parts of an elephant's memory are far better than any other nonhuman animal. When you see the elephant throughout the pages, let it remind you that you have the strength to be compassionate, caring, and calm, and that your experiences and memories matter.

Discover journaling!

Journaling is pretty much just writing your thoughts on paper. It's a great way of reflecting on things that have happened, creating new ideas, or recording your memories. There's no right or wrong way to do it!

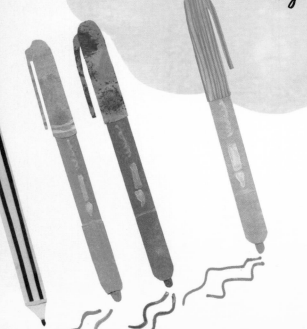

Why journal?

When you start a journal, decide what you'd like to get out of it. Do you want to keep note of your daily doings? Would you like a place to put your hopes and dreams? Do you want to get your thoughts out of your head and come back to them later? You can make lists, write, draw, cut, paste—anything you like!

GETTING STARTED

All you really need to start is something to write with, such as a pen, pencil, or colorful marker, and something to write on, such as a notebook, cute journal, or even just a spare sheet of paper.

Use lots of different colors if you like.

YOUR JOURNAL JOURNEY

Journal however often feels good to you. Whether it's every single day or just once in a while, journaling can help you look at your life in a different way. You might find that it helps you solve problems or feel calm.

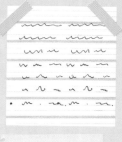

You can draw your ideas, too!

Record your memories in your journal.

How to journal

How do you want your life to unfold? Creating a journal might help you find out. Think of it as a way to help you organize, categorize, and express your thoughts. Don't worry about your writing being perfect. Simply let your ideas flow onto the page.

JOURNALING FOR YOUR MIND

Creating a journal can help you feel less stressed or anxious, and allows you to express your emotions. You might find that writing down your problems makes them feel less big, too.

Types of journals:

BULLET JOURNALS

Bullet journals are a mix between a regular journal and a to-do list. They are based around jotting down short bullet points rather than writing long sentences. If this appeals, you can buy pre-made bullet journals or create one of your own using a blank notebook. There are a lot of resources on the internet to help you get started.

PLANNERS

Planners come in all shapes and sizes. Usually, they are pre-printed with dates or calendars. They often guide you with themes, or help you with a specific area such as school, sports, or keeping track of chores.

JOURNALS

Journals can be lined or completely blank on the inside. Some people choose to simply write in them, but you could sketch, color, or even glue pictures inside. The best thing about a blank journal is that you can make it whatever you want it to be.

Plan new memories to make, too!

Memory scrapbook

Photos help us remember life's special moments. It's handy to be able to see your snapshots at the touch of a button, but nothing beats flicking through a handmade scrapbook of memories.

Leafing through a scrapbook is a fun way to remind yourself of happy memories, but you can find joy in crafting one, too! You can decorate it however you like—it's nice to fill the pages with photos, stickers, and patterned papers that match the theme of the photos.

Choose one or two photos of moments that mean a lot to you and print them out. Take a look at the photos closely. Were they taken on a birthday, holiday, or vacation? Once you've figured out the "theme" of your photos, head to your local craft store or search around your house for stickers, colored or patterned paper, and any other decorations you'd like that fit your theme.

Making your scrapbook

Now it's time to gather your supplies. As well as your photos, stickers, and other decorative items, you'll need glue or double-sided tape and scissors. Be careful when using scissors since they are sharp.

You could use a piece of scrapbooking paper (patterned or plain cardstock) as your base, or just start sticking straight into your book. Make sure the paper is heavy enough that it can have lots of pieces stuck to it!

GET DECORATING!

You can take it in any direction you like. You could use alphabet stickers to spell out a word or phrase that matches the feeling in your photos, or find cute stickers and cut out shapes to arrange around the page to highlight the theme.

Experiment, have fun, and enjoy reliving your happy memories. If you make mistakes, don't worry. It's all part of the creative process.

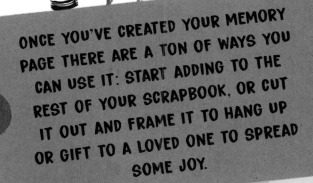

ONCE YOU'VE CREATED YOUR MEMORY PAGE THERE ARE A TON OF WAYS YOU CAN USE IT: START ADDING TO THE REST OF YOUR SCRAPBOOK, OR CUT IT OUT AND FRAME IT TO HANG UP OR GIFT TO A LOVED ONE TO SPREAD SOME JOY.

When you look at a photo, try to remember the moment it was taken.

Cherishing every day with mindfulness

When there are lots of things you need to do, you can forget to live in the moment. Being mindful means taking time to notice things around you, such as the smiles of friends, the taste of food, and the sound of birds. Doing this can make you feel calm and happy.

PAUSE

When you catch yourself feeling overwhelmed or stressed, it helps to pause. Take a few deep breaths in, and slowly let them out each time. Often when things feel chaotic or stressful, you will feel better if you take a moment to slow down.

How to be mindful

Focus your attention on what you are doing at this very moment.
Close your eyes and listen to your breath. Take time to notice your senses:
what can you hear, see, smell, taste, and feel?

YOU CAN DO ALL THESE THINGS MINDFULLY:

BRUSHING YOUR TEETH

WASHING YOUR FACE

GETTING DRESSED

WALKING THE DOG

WRITING IN A JOURNAL

MAKING A DRINK

LISTENING TO MUSIC

When you are doing everyday things such as brushing your teeth, try to focus on what you are doing rather than letting your mind wander. Think about what you can sense. How does the toothpaste taste? How do the bristles feel on your teeth? You can do most everyday things mindfully. When you're eating, focus on the textures and tastes of your food. When you're getting dressed, think about how the clothes feel on your skin. Mindfulness takes practice, but if you try to do it often, you should feel happier and more relaxed.

EATING BREAKFAST

CARING FOR PLANTS

EATING LUNCH

Doing things mindfully will help you remember them.

Body scanning

When did you last take some time for yourself? With so much going on around us, it is easy to feel overwhelmed and stressed. Meditation is a wonderful way of checking in with yourself, and to feel peaceful and calm. It should relax your body and focus your mind.

WHAT IS MEDITATION?

Meditation is a way of deep thinking that calms the body and mind. People often think meditation is sitting silently trying not to think, but it's more about being aware of your body and breathing, and reflecting on yourself and the world around you.

In meditation, you take long, deep breaths and concentrate as each one goes in and out. If your mind wanders, gently focus back on your breath. It sounds like a simple thing to do, but meditation is a skill that requires patient practice. It can teach you to stay in the moment, improve your focus, and give you a positive perspective on your problems. It has even been proven to help you sleep better and improve your memory.

HISTORY OF MEDITATION

Humans have been meditating for more than 7,000 years. Archaeologists believe that many different civilizations, from Japan to Egypt to India, practiced meditation as part of different religions. These days, meditation is practiced by lots of different people, and not just for religious reasons. You can also learn this incredible skill and enjoy its benefits—meditation is for everyone.

Body scanning activity

You just need a few minutes to try this meditation technique, called a "body scan." It's a great way to feel calm and focused.

1.

Sit somewhere quiet and comfortable. Close your eyes.

2.

Take a few long, deep breaths. With each breath, straighten your back and relax your shoulders. Try to relax as much as possible. Release any tension from your face, neck, and mouth.

3.

Imagine a small, soft light about the size of a firefly at the top of your head.

4.

Imagine the light is slowly moving down your body. As it touches each part of your body, check in with that part. Does it feel stiff? Tense? Relaxed? Take your time to connect with each part and stretch it if it feels good.

5.

When you get to your hands, how do they feel? It might feel good to wiggle your fingers. Do the same with your toes.

6.

Once you've scanned all the way down your body, take a moment to check in with yourself. How do you feel? Better than before? Are you happier and more relaxed?

Meditation sharpens your memory.

Breathing colors

Different colors can represent different emotions, and can improve your mood. Think of a color that represents how you'd like to feel. Sit comfortably and breathe deeply. Picture being bathed in a cloud of your color. As you breathe in, imagine breathing in the color and it spreading good feelings through your whole body.

Yellow

Yellow is the color of sunshine. When you need a confidence boost, thinking about yellow might help you feel more vibrant and positive. What does yellow remind you of?

Here are some of the ways colors might make you feel.

Orange

For some people, orange represents creativity, so imagine breathing in the color orange when you need a burst of inspiration. When do you feel most inspired?

Pink

When you need some love and compassion it might help to think about the color pink. How does it make you feel? Can you think of things you can do to love yourself?

Green

The color of plants and nature can represent growth and new beginnings. Thinking of it might help you start something new or grow. What does green mean to you?

Blue

When you want to feel calm and collected, you could picture the vast ocean and let the color blue wash over you. Can you help others feel calm too? How does blue make you feel?

Red

For many, red represents passion and courage. Imagine breathing it in when you want to take action or need a burst of energy. What makes you feel passionate and strong?

Colors might remind you of certain memories, too.

Making mandalas

Have you ever found yourself doodling or creating patterns when you feel stressed or unhappy? Steady, repetitve activities such as drawing or crafting can be very calming. Making a mandala is a good one to try.

WHAT IS A MANDALA?

Mandalas are patterns, usually in the shape of a circle, that are meant to represent the universe. Making them or looking at them once they are finished can help to focus your thoughts or meditate.

MANDALA METHODS

From painting onto cloth or paper to fashioning designs in metal or stone, people use all sorts of methods to create mandalas. Some, like these Buddhist monks, spend many hours or days making them using colored sand. First, they map out the elaborate design in chalk, and then they use tools to precisely and delicately lay the sand in place.

Make one yourself!

You can draw or paint a mandala onto paper, or try making one out of objects you've found in nature. Sketch a circular design on some paper or cardstock, then lay your objects in place. Try to make the pattern symmetrical, but don't worry if it isn't perfect. While making your mandala, try to clear your head of stressful thoughts and instead enjoy watching the patterns build up in front of you.

1

Begin at the center.

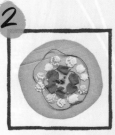

2

Try to make your design symmetrical.

3

Build up the design row by row.

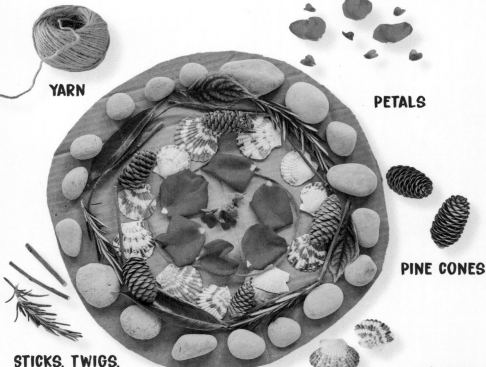

YARN

PETALS

PINE CONES

STICKS, TWIGS, AND LEAVES

PEBBLES

SHELLS

Use any materials you like to create your mandala. See what you can find around your home or outside. Items such as buttons, coins, or beads work well, too!

MANDALA MINDFULNESS

While you create your mandala, try to relax. Soften your jaw and shoulders, and take long, deep breaths. Focus on how each object feels in your hand and place it with care and precision. Think about how your mandala makes you feel.

What does your mandala mean to you?

Relaxing origami

Working with your hands can be satisfying and calming. Origami, the art of paper folding, is a great way to relax while also creating something beautiful.

ORIGAMI ORIGINS

Historians don't know exactly when origami began. It was first written about in the 1600s in Japan when it was a popular hobby. Origami models are usually of animals, plants, or other things from nature, and are made from just a small piece of paper. However, some incredible artists make origami sculptures larger than a person using a single giant piece of paper!

PRACTICE MAKES PERFECT

Origami takes patience, intention, and attention. Your creations may not turn out exactly the way they appear in the instructions, but that's okay! The more you practice, the better you'll become.

Tie a piece of thread to your paper cranes and hang them in your room.

ORIGAMI INSPIRATION

You might have tried origami before—perhaps making a paper plane to fly across a room or a boat to float in a pond. With a little practice, you will be able to create more complicated designs. You could try folding beautiful flowers such as roses and lotuses or making lots of different origami animals to create your own zoo! The options are endless.

CRAFTING A CRANE

To make an origami crane (a type of bird), all you need is a square piece of paper and a flat surface, such as a table. Take your time with your folds, pressing them down firmly so they are neat and precise. Concentrating on each fold will help you clear your mind and forget your worries.

1

Fold it in half diagonally one way and unfold. Then fold in half the other way and unfold, making creases as the dotted lines show.

2

Flip the paper over and fold it in half horizontally and vertically along the lines shown, unfolding each time.

3

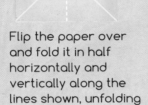

Turn the paper to make a diamond. Pull the left and right corners into the middle and down to the bottom corner. Your paper should fold into a square. Squash it flat.

4

Keeping the flappy end at the bottom, fold the edge of each side of the top flap inward to meet the center line. Unfold. Flip the paper over and repeat on the other side.

5

Fold the top triangle toward you to make a crease. Unfold it. Lift up the top flap from the bottom and fold it back over the top triangle.

6

The sides should fold in to meet the center line. Flatten this down into a diamond. Flip the paper over and fold the top triangle toward you. Unfold and repeat step 6 on this side.

7

Fold both sides of the top flaps of paper along the lines shown above. They should meet at the center. Turn over and repeat on the other side.

8

You should now have a long, thin kite shape. Take one side of the kite and flatten it out so you can fold its leg upward.

9

Then press it down so the leg is pointing out to the side and tucked in between one side of the kite.

10

BEAK

Repeat on the other side, to create two sticking out legs. Fold down the top of one of the legs to make the crane's head.

11

WINGS

FOLD DOWN

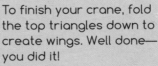

To finish your crane, fold the top triangles down to create wings. Well done—you did it!

PAPER CRANE!

As you make each fold, think of something you are grateful for.

Vision board

Visualizing your wildest wishes in your mind and on paper is a powerful way to keep your goals in focus. You can try making a vision board to do this!

WHY MAKE A VISION BOARD?

Do you have dreams and goals for your future? Or are you not sure what they look like for you yet? As you make your way through life, you'll experience so much amazing growth and change. It's important to embrace the changes you can't control, but also to take control of those you can.

Creating a vision board is a great way to think about what you might want to achieve in your life. It's a collection of pictures, magazine clippings, photos, and words that you can use to inspire yourself about future hopes, plans, and dreams.

WHAT IS YOUR VISION FOR THE FUTURE?

Making a vision board is an enjoyable form of self-care, and it can help you at times in your life when you have to make decisions.

1 Close your eyes. Think about what you'd like to see happen in your life. Don't limit yourself to what you think is realistic—let your imagination run wild.

2 Now get to work on your vision board! Start by flicking through used magazines and newspapers. Carefully cut out words or pictures that inspire you. As you gather materials, try to keep an open mind about what you include.

3 Themes might form in what you gather. Perhaps you've cut out scenes from different countries because you're seeking adventure. Maybe you've been drawn to words about friendship that inspire you to be a better friend. Think about the links between the things you've chosen.

4 Find a notebook or piece of cardstock or paper. Arrange your clippings on the page. You might want to put a picture of your biggest goal or a motivational word at the center. Enjoy playing with moving the clippings around the page. Then, when you're happy, stick them all down!

5 Decorate your vision board. You could add ribbons, stickers, or pieces of colorful wrapping paper. Or you might use paints and pens to add more color. Do whatever you want—it's your vision after all!

What on your vision board will end up being a memory?

Lists and mindmaps

When life gets busy and overwhelming, it can be difficult to know how to break down your tasks and problems. Pick up a pen and a notebook or journal, and let's begin!

LISTS

One of the best ways to get organized is to write a list. Whether you want to get on top of a mountain of schoolwork, or break down how you're going to achieve a goal, making a list is an easy way to tidy your thoughts. It might help to work backward: what's your end goal and what do you need to do to get there? Color-code tasks with pens, then check them off as you achieve each one. It's okay if you don't check them all off in one day— there's always tomorrow!

Mindmaps

A fun and creative way to organize your ideas is to put them into a mindmap. It can help you get jumbled thoughts out of your head and onto paper. All you need is a problem you want to solve or a goal you want to achieve, and blank piece of paper and some colored pens or pencils.

PICK UP A NEW HOBBY

SPEND TIME IN NATURE

SEE FRIENDS

MY SUMMER VACATION GOALS

MAKE TIME FOR MUSIC

BE HEALTHY

PLAY SPORTS

Add pictures to each thought or task to help you remember them.

MAKE YOUR MINDMAP

Write your goal in the middle of your paper and circle it. Draw branches from it, and write different tasks or problems along each branch. Organize your ideas into groups, giving each group a different color. Add branches to each branch if you like!

Use mindmaps to plan things you'll remember forever.

Calming mark making

Making simple, repetitive marks on paper can be very therapeutic. Using a brush with ink or paint feels lovely. Different types of pencils and pens might inspire you to make different patterns. But you can use anything to make marks! Get creative!

ANCIENT INSPIRATION

The ink brush was invented in China around 300 BCE. Perhaps you've seen Chinese calligraphy, which uses brush strokes and ink to depict characters. Even though this style of writing was created long ago, people still use a similar technique today! It can be a really calming and enjoyable activity.

INK BRUSHES

MAKE YOUR OWN MARK MAKER

BRUSHES

Start with a simple brush you already own, such as a paintbrush. Or make your own by tying twigs of plants such as rosemary onto sturdy sticks. Experiment with different materials to make different marks.

BUBBLE WRAP

Try dipping bubble wrap into paint for a textured effect.

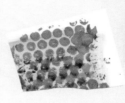

Mark making techniques

Start by trying single strokes and then experiment with different types of lines, loops, and circles. Use different amounts of pressure and hold your mark maker at different angles for different effects. Here are some ideas to try:

CALM BRUSH MARKS

PENCIL SQUIGGLES

BRUSH SQUIGGLES

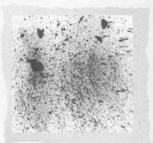

PAINT SPLATTERS

THIN BRUSH MARKS

CROSS HATCHING

INKY MARKS

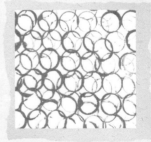

CIRCLES

Try cutting your marked paper into shapes or use it for crafts!

Some mark makers may hold memories.

MESSY DRAWER, MESSY MIND!

Tidy room, tidy mind

Keeping calm is hard to do if the space around you is chaotic. We often fill our lives with things we don't need. Clearing your space of things that don't bring you joy can help you tidy your mind, as well as your room!

Give things a second life

Surrounding yourself with things that make you feel happy can help you feel relaxed, and keeping things that don't can feel stressful. If you keep a sweater that doesn't fit or feel right, you can end up feeling guilty that you're not wearing it. But don't throw it away—give it a second life! Gift unwanted items to friends or donate them to charity. It's better for the environment, and when you release things that don't bring you happiness, you'll have more space for the things that do.

COLOR-CODE AND CATEGORIZE!

How do you keep things neat?

Don't wait until your room is a mess to tidy it!
Build daily habits to keep it ordered.

MAKE

COLORFUL

PEGGED

REMINDERS!

Take your time

The longer you put off tidying, the harder it will be to do, so do it now! Set aside some time to work through your room bit by bit. As you pick up each thing, take a moment to enjoy how it makes you feel and think about what joy it brings. Does it bring up any memories?

A place for everything

Decide on a "home" for each of your things. When everything has its own place, finding and storing it is a breeze.

PAINTED JAR TIDY POTS

1

PAINT THE JARS

Rainbow order is a fun way to organize. Paint old jars each color of the rainbow.

2

ARRANGE BY COLOR

Categorize your stationery or school supplies and have a jar for each category. You could put your crayons in one jar and your coloring pens in another. This will make them much easier to find!

Your space will hold many memories—cherish them!

Finding your space

When things get too much, going to a place that makes you feel better is good for your mental health. Your space could be a park, the beach, the library, or even just a nice corner of your house. Think about a place that makes you feel safe, calm, and happy. Why does it make you feel that way?

IF YOU FEEL DOWN, GOING   TO A SPECIAL PLACE

HOW TO FIND YOUR SPACE

Close your eyes and think of a place that lifts your mood. If nowhere springs to mind, that's okay! Use this as a chance to explore around you. Once you've found your space, you could use it to do a hobby, such as a sport, reading, or simply sitting and observing what's around you.

READING BOOKS

HAPPY SLEEP-SPACE

Making the space where you sleep feel calm is good, too! You could put up photos of good memories or decorate in your favorite color. Try to keep electronic devices like phones out of this space since they can cause you to sleep badly. Keep a book beside your bed for bedtime reading instead.

OBSERVING NATURE

DOING A SPORT

Take a picture of your safe space to put on your wall.

CAN HELP TO LIFT   **YOUR MOOD.**

Plants and growth

One of the most amazing things about being alive is how we grow and change every day. Caring for plants can remind us of this growth, since they grow and change every day, too. Start your own indoor garden with some of these easy-to-grow plants.

Use the ideas on this page to get inspiration for your own home garden!

CHINESE MONEY PLANT

SPIDER PLANT

Some plants love to be up high. Get some pots (thrift stores are a great place to find them) and ask a grown-up to help you hang them from a high spot. Experiment with hanging them at different heights.

Keep your own plants!

Marigolds

These flowers are usually red, orange, or yellow. Some cultures consider them good luck. Their smell repels certain insects that might try to eat your other plants.

Spider plants

These plants are named for their long, snakelike leaves. They are very easy to grow and sprout new little plants from the end of their stalks!

Cacti and succulents

These low-effort plants are easy if you don't have a green thumb. They don't need much water to survive and they thrive in natural light.

African violets

These flowers come in many colors, from white and pink to red and purple. They love bright spots so would be perfect to grow on a sunny windowsill!

PROPAGATE YOUR PLANTS!

With some types of plants, you can grow new plants from your big plant. This is called propagation. To propagate a Chinese money plant, gently pull away one of the smaller offshoots growing around it. You might need to untangle the roots.

Plant your little offshoot in a small pot with some potting soil. Always wash your hands well after touching soil.

WATCH IT GROW!

Now just find a sunny spot for your plant, water it when the soil is dry, and wait. Slowly, the offshoot should grow its own roots and new leaves should start to grow.

Scientists have evidence that talking to plants nicely can help them grow. After complimenting your plants, say a few nice things to yourself, too.

Remember to water your plants!

Let's get outside

Is your head feeling overwhelmed? Here's what you're going to do: open your front door to let the air in, take a big deep breath, and get outside! Just a few minutes in the fresh air can boost your mood and your energy.

Take a walk

Walking in nature is really good for your body and your mind! Breathe deeply and be present in the moment. Use your senses to take in what's around you. What can you hear? What can you smell? Look around and try to really take in the colors, shapes, and sizes of what you see.

Run your fingers over the knobbles of a pine cone or the smooth head of an acorn.

Observe the different shapes of leaves on the trees. Do you know what kind they are?

Are the leaves fresh and green, or are they turning yellow and drifting to the ground?

Take joy from the bright colors and sweet scents of flowers and plants.

HAVE YOU EVER TAKEN A BATH IN THE FOREST?

Find some woods, a forest, or a park, and simply be calm and quiet among the trees. In Japan, they call this shinrin yoku, which means "forest bathing." Always ask your grown-up before you go wandering.

Make a nature journal

Write a list of what you enjoy about being outside, such as how the breeze feels on your face. Note what you have seen, draw pictures, or even stick found objects such as leaves and flowers onto the pages.

Remember with your nature journal.

Nature is so beautiful!

Wonderful wildlife

Exploring nature can be calming and inspiring. It's nice to discover it outside in the fresh air, but even just spending a few minutes looking out of a window can be wonderful. Perhaps there's wildlife you see every day but don't pause to notice.

PAINTED PEBBLE MEMORIES

It's nice to have memories of your time in nature. Collect interesting things from the ground to remember your time in a certain place. They could be fun fallen leaves, amazing shells, or exciting rocks. Make your very own natural souvenirs by finding lovely, smooth pebbles. Paint them with things you'd like to remember from that place such as flowers or animals.

Nature notes

It's fun to observe the creatures you see. There are so many animals out there, but we don't often take the time to really watch them. Whether it's squirrels scuffling in your yard, a robin singing as the sun rises, or a hummingbird fluttering its wings outside your window, take joy in the world around you.

Sketch your surroundings

Drawing or painting what you can see around you is a nice way of remembering wildlife—perhaps you want to remember a particularly beautiful day or an interesting species you spotted. If you'd prefer to write, use the journaling tips in this book to guide you instead.

KEEPING TRACK OF NATURE MIGHT HELP YOU TO NOTICE MORE!

WILDLIFE LISTS

It's fun keeping a list of wildlife you see out and about. It might help you tune in with your surroundings and see more. Take note of distinctive things, such as markings, that mean you could spot the same animal again. Keep note of how many of each thing you spot. Then next time you go out, you can see if the numbers have changed.

Nature is one of the nicest places to make memories!

Yoga fun

We spend a lot of the day sitting down, which can leave our bodies feeling tired and stiff. It's important to move your body to combat these feelings, and to take care of your mental health, too. Yoga is a great activity that stretches your body, makes you strong, and works out your mind!

BREATHING

When doing your yoga poses, don't forget to breathe! Try to focus on breathing slowly and deeply.

As you breathe in, feel your chest and stomach rise as they fill with air. As you breathe out, feel them go down.

See if you can match your breaths to your movements, breathing in as you adjust your position, and breathing out as you stretch.

Make a mental note of how breathing makes you feel. Focusing on your breathing can make you feel calm, or perhaps you will feel energized. It will depend on your mood.

Give it a try!

You can practice yoga almost anywhere, and almost anybody can do it. No one knows your body like you do, so when you try a pose, listen to your body. If it feels wrong or painful, stop! If it feels good, keep it up! Here are some poses to try:

CHILD'S POSE

Kneel with your feet together and knees apart. Stretch yourself forward with your hands flat on the floor. Enjoy the stretch through your back. If it's comfortable, rest your forehead on the floor. Breathe deeply.

CHAIR POSE

Stand with your back against a wall and your feet and knees slightly apart. Slowly bend your knees, sliding your back down the wall until you reach a sitting position. Your legs should form a square and your back should be flat against the wall.

Don't use a mat for this since it could slip!

Look at something that isn't moving if you feel wobbly.

TREE POSE

Stand up straight with your feet together and eyes ahead. Keep one foot on the floor and lift the other up so it rests on your leg above or below your knee—NEVER on your knee. Stretch your arms above your head.

WARRIOR POSE

Stand with your legs wide. Turn your left leg out. Bend your left knee deeply and stretch your arms out wide. Keep your body straight, but turn your head to look at your left fingers. Repeat on the other side.

Do them often, and your body will remember the poses.

Understanding emotions

Feelings and emotions affect everything. Having them is part of being human, so it's good to understand them! Emotions begin in your brain and affect how you react to different situations. Many scientists think that most of our feelings come from one of four basic emotions: happiness, anger, fear, or sadness.

MAKE AN EMOTIONS WHEEL

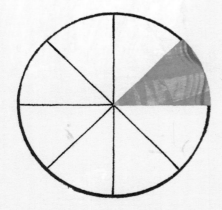

This activity can be used to express yourself or see the range of emotions that you have. Draw a circle and divide it into eight sections. Label each section with the emotions in the diagram to the right. When you are feeling that way, decorate that section of the diagram with patterns and colors that match your mood. How are the colors and patterns different from mood to mood?

HAPPY
SAD
ANGRY
EXCITED
SURPRISED
PROUD
SCARED
WORRIED

All feelings are important

No feeling is "good" or "bad."
Some are light and gentle while
others are strong and powerful.
All feelings are important. Everyone
has all sorts of different emotions,
and they make you who you are.
Don't be afraid to show them!

YOUR LITTLE EMOTIONS BOX

You might find that some objects can
help when you're feeling a certain
way. Perhaps you feel cheered up by
fiddling with your favorite beads, or
you are soothed when you hold a
smooth, cool pebble you found at the
beach. Here's a way to make a little
box to keep your precious things in
for when you need them most.

1

Take a square piece
of paper. Fold it in
half horizontally and
vertically along the
folds above, unfolding
it each time.

2

Flip the paper over.
Fold the corners of the
paper into the middle
of the square to form a
smaller square.

3

Fold the top and
bottom sides into the
middle of the paper to
meet the center
crease and unfold.

4

Then fold the left
and right sides to
meet the middle
crease of the paper,
too, and unfold.

5

Unfold the left and
right triangles that
are pointing into the
center, too.

6

Fold the top and bottom sides
into the middle again.

7

Grab one triangle
and pull it up and inward
so a square box pops up.
Pull the other triangle
inward too.

8

AND YOU HAVE A BOX!

Fold the triangles down into the box, making
sure all the folds are nice and sharp so they
stay in place. Use a bit of tape or glue to
stick them down, if needed.

Your memories are filled
with emotions, too.

GLUE STICK

Gratitude practice

Taking time to feel grateful for the things you have (and the things you don't) can help you feel happy, energized, and less stressed. The more you focus on good things, the more positive you will feel.

BE GRATEFUL FOR YOU!

It's also important to be grateful to your wonderful self. The way you talk to and think about yourself is very powerful, so be kind to yourself and think about what makes you so great!

How to practice gratitude

KEEP A GRATITUDE JOURNAL

When you wake up each morning, write down three things you are grateful for. They can be anything you like: small or big, general or specific. At the end of the day, write down three more things. When you're feeling low, look back at your list to remind you of what makes you grateful.

Make a colorful card to write your notes on!

WRITE A THANK YOU NOTE

It's lovely to write thank you cards to friends and family. The cards don't have to be for receiving a gift— sometimes the most thoughtful cards are are the ones that tell someone why you appreciate them and remind them of memories you've shared together.

MAKE A GRATITUDE JAR

On little pieces of colored paper, write down good memories or things that have happened that you are grateful for. Put them into a jar to dip into for memories of good times and to remind you to practice gratitude.

I AM SO LUCKY!

Be grateful for your memories!

You could even share your notes with family and friends so you can remember together.

Glossary

anxiety
Feeling tense, worried, or stressed

calligraphy
Handwritten lettering

compassion
Having sympathy for the feelings of others

gratitude
Being thankful for something

intention
An aim or plan

journaling
Writing in a journal or diary

meditation
A calming practice that focuses the mind

mental health
How you feel emotionally

mindmap
A diagram to help you organize information

perspective
A point of view on something

propagation
Growing a new plant from a bigger plant

self-care
Looking after yourself physically and mentally

symmetrical
A shape with two matching parts

therapeutic
Having a pleasant effect on your body or your mind

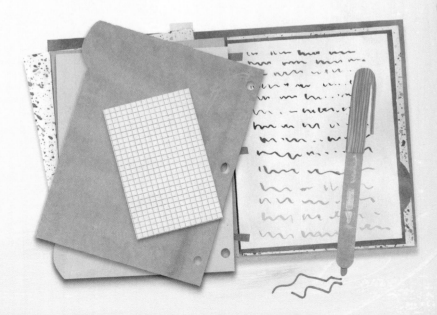

Index

Acknowledgments

The publishers would like to thank Helen Peters for the index, Sonny Flynn and Charlotte Milner for their design help, and Jack Whyte, Hanna Bollito, and Hiromi Watanabe for their origami expertise.

The publisher would like to thank the following for their kind permission to reproduce their photographs:

(Key: a-above; b-below/bottom; c-center; f-far; l-left; r-right; t-top)

16 Dreamstime.com: Mikhail Avdeev (cr).
20 Dreamstime.com: Iphotothailand (cr).
28 Alamy Stock Photo: Jeremy Sutton-Hibbert (bl)

All other images © Dorling Kindersley
For further information see:
www.dkimages.com